C000080817

BOOK ANALYSIS

Written by Camilo Casallas Torres
Translated by Emma Hanna

A Confederacy of Dunces

BY JOHN KENNEDY TOOLE

Bright
≡Summaries.com

JOHN KENNEDY TOOLE

AMERICAN NOVELIST

- **Born in New Orleans in 1937.**
- **Died in Biloxi (Mississippi) in 1969.**
- **Literary awards:**
  - Pulitzer Prize for Fiction, 1981 (for *A Confederacy of Dunces*; awarded posthumously)
- **Notable works:**
  - *A Confederacy of Dunces* (1980), novel
  - *The Neon Bible* (1989), novel

John Kennedy Toole grew up in a middle-class environment which afforded him very few opportunities to exercise his creativity and often left him feeling suffocated. His mother was unable to help him overcome these issues, and he had a complex relationship with her: although they were very close, their relationship was characterised by conflict and rejection. However, she was the one who first introduced him to the world of art and literature by enrolling him in a comedic theatre class.

Kennedy Toole later attended Tulane University, after which he went on to study English at Colombia University. He also taught several university-level classes, and was fairly well-respected in the academic world. However, his career was interrupted when he was drafted into military service and deployed to Puerto Rico, although he continued teaching English Literature during his time there.

After completing *A Confederacy of Dunces*, Kennedy Toole submitted the manuscript to a number of publishers, but it was rejected every time. This left Kennedy Toole feeling depressed, paranoid and shut out of the literary world, and he decided to travel around the United States. After arriving in Biloxi, Mississippi, he committed suicide by connecting a hosepipe to his car's exhaust pipe and inhaling the carbon monoxide.

A decade later, his mother gave a copy of the manuscript of *A Confederacy of Dunces* to the publisher Walker Percy, as he recounts in his foreword to the novel:

> "But the lady was persistent, and it somehow came to pass that she stood in my office handing

me the hefty manuscript. There was no getting out of it; only one hope remained – that I could read a few pages and that they would be bad enough for me, in good conscience, to read no farther.

[...]

In this case I read on. And on. First with the sinking feeling that it was not bad enough to quit, then with a prickle of interest, then a growing excitement, and finally an incredulity: surely it was not possible that it was so good." (pp. vii-viii)

Kennedy Toole's mother was therefore the one who eventually catapulted him to fame.

EARLY EFFORTS

Kennedy Toole only ever wrote one other novel: *The Neon Bible*. It is set in an ordinary American town during the Second World War, and centres on a reclusive teenager who lives with his mother and aunt. All the men in the town have left to fight in the war, and all the women have gone to work in the factories. Any men who come back from the war become either religious fanatics or alcoholics, and the protagonist tries to escape this life.

Kennedy Toole came to hate this novel, which he considered excessively juvenile, and never seriously attempted to get it published. Although *A Confederacy of Dunces* is widely accepted to be his masterpiece, *The Neon Bible* is also worthy of critical recognition.

A CONFEDERACY OF DUNCES

A TALE ABOUT SOCIETY'S UNDERBELLY

- **Genre:** picaresque novel
- **Reference edition:** Kennedy Toole, J. (1987) *A Confederacy of Dunces*. New York: Grove Weidenfeld.
- **1st edition:** 1980
- **Themes:** alienation, poverty, work, politics

A Confederacy of Dunces is a fascinatingly unusual novel. It was so unique for its time that Walker Percy even commented on the responsible way it addressed racial tensions, eschewing stereotypes and the contradictory stances on these issues that still plagued the country's political landscape.

The novel's protagonist is Ignatius J. Reilly, an eccentric, ostentatious character who lives in New Orleans. He blindly believes in the benefits of a monarchy as a system of government and in medieval philosophy, and he therefore considers himself a bastion of morality. He fights constantly with his mother, who makes him take on a variety of menial jobs, where his implacable moral beliefs lead him to influence, annoy and scorn his employers and colleagues.

Eventually, the cycle of confrontations that has come to define Ignatius's life becomes unsustainable, which has a marked effect on both his physical appearance and his beliefs.

SUMMARY

A DECADENT PARTY IN NEW ORLEANS

Ignatius J. Reilly is patiently waiting for his mother to finish her shopping when a police officer called Angelo Mancuso suddenly begins questioning him, because Ignatius's comical hunting cap, ridiculous moustache and tremendous obesity make him seem like a suspicious character. Ignatius is saved by Claude Robichaux, an elderly man obsessed with communism, who thinks that the policeman is bothering Ignatius and attacks him. A few moments later, Ignatius's mother Irene arrives, and the two of them leave while Mancuso arrests Robichaux.

The Reillys end up in a strip club called Night of Joy. They are acquainted with Darlene, one of the waitresses who works there, and her tyrannical boss Lana Lee, and chat to both women. However, Ignatius's presence makes the bar's other customers feel very uncomfortable, as he keeps burping and smells very bad.

After leaving the bar, Ignatius and Irene look for their car amid all the hustle and bustle of New Orleans, where the sweltering streets are full of drunkards and partygoers in full costume. They find the car and Irene gets into the driver's seat, but she has had too much to drink and crashes the car in front of a building. The owner comes out to yell at the Reillys, but Mancuso arrives on the scene and manages to defuse the situation before it gets any worse. However, he tells them that they will have to pay the owner for the damages.

SETTING THE SCENE

A Confederacy of Dunces has been lauded for more than just its comedic touches; it is also widely regarded as an exceptionally comprehensive overview of all the social groups living in New Orleans and their unique ways of speaking, as the novel's characters include policemen, working-class labourers, prostitutes, and people from the city's black, Italian, Irish and Latino communities, among others. The novel's epigraph even claims that New Orleans has more in common with the coastal cities of the Mediterranean than with cities like New York. While it is not the main subject of the novel, the city's cosmopolitan and multicultural character nevertheless plays an important secondary role in it.

THE PATRON SAINT OF LOST CAUSES

Now that the family has been saddled with a large debt, Irene tells her son that he will have to get a job. Ignatius initially refuses, as he believes that he is better suited to spirituality, intellectualism, writing and watching television than working a normal job, but he eventually agrees, and starts looking for work. In the end, he gets a job at Levy Pants, a company which produces jeans. Ignatius's job involves managing the company archives, but he also embarks on an ethical crusade to improve the way the company works. The company is mostly run by Gonzalez, a mediocre but punctual office manager, and Miss Trixie, an eccentric secretary, while the owner is almost entirely uninvolved. Ignatius tries to persuade the black factory workers to protest against the boss, Mr Levy, and eventually convinces them by performing a ridiculous dance in front of them. He also sends a letter full of insults to one of the company's suppliers and forges Mr Levy's signature at the bottom of it. Meanwhile, the workers learn that Ignatius once had a run-in with the police and lose faith in him, so the protest is cancelled. Ignatius is fired shortly afterwards.

At this point, the reader learns that Ignatius had a strange relationship with a left-wing Jewish woman called Myrna Minkoff while he was at university. Paradoxically, their relationship was fuelled by their utterly antithetical worldviews, but it eventually came to an end: Myrna is now an activist and lives in New York, while Ignatius still lives with his mother and is becoming increasingly reclusive. Ignatius wants to provoke Myrna, so he sends her letters telling her that he is spearheading a workers' protest.

THE WHEEL OF FORTUNE

Mancuso's superiors lambast him after he arrests Robichaux, and he is ordered to dress up in ridiculous costumes (such as Santa Claus) and wander around the city in order to attract and catch delinquents. Following the accident, Irene becomes friends with the police officer and his aunt, Santa Battaglia. Ignatius believes that this relationship is toxic, because when they go out bowling together they end up drinking heavily and staying out until the early hours of the morning. Furthermore, Santa disapproves of Ignatius because she believes that he takes advantage of Irene.

Nevertheless, when his mother asks him to lend the policeman a copy of his favourite book, Ignatius agrees. The book in question is *The Consolation of Philosophy* by Boethius (Roman philosopher, c. 480-524), and discusses the author's belief that the world is against him.

A MEDIEVAL MAN

Ignatius's personal philosophy is entirely based on a complex medieval system of thought, and draws particularly heavily on the writings of Boethius. Accordingly, the quintessential medieval image of the Wheel of Fortune appears frequently throughout the book, and is portrayed as a powerful force which turns inexorably onwards while humans are left at the mercy of its whims.

| The Wheel of Fortune

A young black man called Jones is released
from prison and begins working at the Night of
Joy. Although he believes he is being underpaid
for his work as a cleaner, he feels like he has no
choice but to keep the job, as he is being threate-
ned by the police. Jones decides to sabotage the
business in revenge, and starts keeping a close

eye on the bar's comings and goings. He soon realises that Lana Lee, the owner, is caught up in some shady dealings: he sees her hand over some suspicious-looking packages to a man called Gus, and although she says that it is to help orphans, Jones does not believe her. Gus meets Mancuso in a train station and steals *The Consolation of Philosophy* from him.

PIRATES AND HOT DOGS

Having lost his job at Levy Pants, Ignatius comes under fire from his mother once again, and he starts looking for work again. He finds another job selling hot dogs from a street cart for a company called Paradise Vendors, which requires him to dress up as a pirate, complete with a plastic sword, a red kerchief and a gold earring. The Wheel of Fortune spins on, and Ignatius starts putting on weight because he is eating all the hot dogs, then his supervisor accuses him of being unhygienic because of his habit of petting cats while he works. The supervisor eventually gives him another chance, but he tells Ignatius that from now on he will have to work in the city's red light district. Gus, the man Lana Lee does business with, observes that Ignatius's cart would be perfect for keeping their packages in. Ignatius agrees to transport the packages, but demands payment, and is tremendously moved when he sees that Gus has a copy of *The Consolation of Philosophy* (which is actually his own copy of the book which Gus stole). At that moment, one of the packages breaks, revealing that Gus is a peddler of pornography. Ignatius falls in love with one of the women in the photographs, who looks like a university professor who has been forced to strip. Ignatius demands that Gus introduce him to the professor, and Gus says that she works at Night of Joy. Ignatius immediately swears that he will rescue her from the amoral hell she lives in.

ONE LAST TURN OF THE WHEEL

Later on, Ignatius convinces himself that he will be able to provoke Myrna by founding a political party which solely consists of gay men and women and winning the next election. However, Myrna simply assumes that Ignatius is gay himself, and the political rally is a disaster because the attendees think that it is just a party and throw Ignatius out.

Ignatius heads to Night of Joy, and is followed by a mysterious man in a hat who was also at the rally. Jones, who now works as both a doorman and an actor, lets him in, even though Lana Lee is suspicious. Ignatius is disappointed to realise that the actress onstage is not the woman he was hoping to see, but Darlene. The show comes to an abrupt end when an exotic bird gets caught in Ignatius's gold hoop earring, which gives him such a fright that he loses control, knocks the tables over, crashes out of the building and gets hit by a bus. At that moment, it is revealed that the man in the hat is Mancuso. Jones realises that this is his chance to get revenge, and tells Mancuso to look in the compartment of the hot dog cart where the pornography is hidden.

REBIRTH

Ignatius recovers from the accident and learns that he has become rather infamous, which his mother finds extremely embarrassing; a photo of Ignatius lying spread-eagled on the pavement has even appeared in several newspapers. Around the same time, the letter that Ignatius wrote to the supplier of Levy Pants is discovered, and the supplier sues the company for half a million dollars. Mr Levy is sure that it was Ignatius who really wrote the letter and openly accuses him of doing so, but to his surprise Ignatius lies and says that it was really the half-mad Miss Trixie who sent it. The old woman is so confused that she does not deny the accusation. Even though Mr Levy knows that this story is untrue, he realises that it will benefit everyone involved, as it will allow Miss Trixie to fulfil her dream of retiring, while the debt will still be cancelled and no harm will come to Ignatius.

Irene is tired and worried about her son, and wants to commit Ignatius to an asylum. However, he realises what she has in mind and starts planning to escape. Fortunately, Myrna arrives at just that moment, as she has had a premonition that everything is going wrong. Ignatius gets into Myrna's car, and they drive off just as the ambulance from the asylum arrives. Ignatius feels content.

CHARACTER STUDY

A Confederacy of Dunces brings together a fascinating cast of characters who can best be described as antiheroes, who dwell in squalid apartments and spend their time skulking around the streets of New Orleans. These strange characters bear little resemblance to traditional literary protagonists: they are not beautiful, intelligent heroes, but the dregs of society.

IGNATIUS J. REILLY

Ignatius is an enormous man who is immediately noticeable wherever he goes:

> "A green hunting cap squeezed the top of the fleshy balloon of a head. The green earflaps, full of large ears and uncut hair and the fine bristles that grew in the ears themselves, stuck out on either side like turn signals indicating two directions at once. Full, pursed lips protruded beneath the bushy black moustache and, at their corners, sank into little folds filled with disapproval and potato chip crumbs." (p. 1)

Ignatius utterly defies description. He is a post-modern Don Quixote, a blinkered hero whose belief in and commitment to his outlandish ideals is absolute, a purveyor of the ridiculous with a talent for dancing and disguise, a tremendous glutton with a rapier wit, a friend to the outcasts and an enemy of modernity. In a way, he embodies the best and worst of life in the 20th century: he reads theological treatises and watches the TV programme Yogi Bear with the same fervent attention; he is equally capable of organising strikes for black workers and lambasting the moral decadence of the era he is living in. His personality is riddled with contradictions, and the chaotic workings of his mind are simultaneously terrifying and enthralling. The only things we can be sure of are that he burps constantly and that he is against fascism – he is not the hero we deserve, but the hero we need.

IRENE REILLY

Being Ignatius's mother is no easy task, and it has left Irene disillusioned and fatalistic. She constantly begs Ignatius to change his attitude, and is practically obsessed with his wellbeing, even though he mistreats her. At first glance, Irene seems like a typical housewife, but in reality she has been left a shell of her former self by the death of her husband and her fear of what everyone else thinks of her. She is a solitary person, and guards her few friendships jealously. Although she and Ignatius are close, their relationship is clearly toxic for both of them.

MYRNA MINKOFF

For the majority of the novel, we only get to know Myrna through the emotional letters she writes to Ignatius, begging him to choose a more liberated way of life and to free himself from the provincial city he lives in and from his relationship with Irene. Given that the novel was written during the early days of the hippie movement, Myrna's character could be interpreted as the embodiment of all the influences of the era and the power of a number of disparate mid-century movements, including the civil rights movement, psychoanalysis and leftist economics.

Myrna is Jewish and very liberated, and acts as a foil to Ignatius. His reactionary beliefs and obsession with ethics stands in contrast to Myrna's liberalism, which has allowed her to make a fresh start in New York, surrounded by beatniks and students from all over the world, and to find happiness there. However, they complement each other because they are both fiery revolutionaries who despise dim-wittedness and the mediocrity of the society they live in above all else.

BURMA JONES

Burma Jones represents the outcasts and the poorest members of society in New Orleans. He is a victim of police brutality and spends his time drowning his sorrows in the city's most disreputable bars. Like many of the most downtrodden people in society, Jones is severely underpaid, and is even worse off than most because of the multi-layered oppression he faces: while poor white people also suffer throughout the book, as a black man, Jones's options are limited to working in terrible conditions or being jailed. His character is also notable for the dialect he speaks, which is particular to the inhabitants of New Orleans.

MANCUSO

None of the characters in *A Confederacy of Dunces* are immune to hardship, not even members of the police. Mancuso is an ordinary patrolman who is constantly ridiculed by his superiors, who force him to dress up in ridiculous costumes to catch delinquents, reducing him to nothing more than another of the city's oddities. He is devoted to his job, but is not overly bright, and therefore fits in perfectly with the hordes of fools that populate society.

DARLENE

Darlene dreams of being an exotic dancer, but her current job is nothing more exciting than waitressing. She is good-hearted, and is constantly belittled by her employer, Lana Lee. She is an unusual character, as she dreams of becoming a sex worker who is the object of constant male attention, but this dream is never realised. Like the other characters, Darlene is deeply unhappy because she has been rejected by society, as she wants to be desired but is desired by no one.

ANALYSIS

A picaresque novel

A Confederacy of Dunces is narrated by a detached third person narrator who does not get overly involved with the characters. The narrator's distant tone provides the reader with an objective view of the strange reality these characters live in, and the dryness of this tone serves to accentuate the novel's humorous touches. For example, the battle between Ignatius and his supervisor at Paradise Vendors and the ridiculous dance he performs in front of the black workers at Levy Pants are both described with utter indifference.

These episodes allow the book to be classified as a picaresque novel, which is closely associated with Spanish-language literature. The genre of picaresque fiction emerged in response to the serious, highbrow literature which predominated during the Renaissance, and usually features characters from the lower classes of society who manage to swindle their employers. In fact, the workplace is a common setting for picaresque stories. It also tends to incorporate a great deal of humour related to bodily functions: the characters fart, vomit, eat, fall, brawl and belch constantly. This kind of humour is still popular today in a variety of comic films and TV shows.

Picaresque literature is often viewed as vulgar, but it actually plays a key role in shining a spotlight on the ordinary people who are so often forgotten or sidelined, and it depicts social hierarchies in a highly original manner. In fact, picaresque novels can be interpreted as a criticism of elitism and the unequal distribution of political and economic power.

A Confederacy of Dunces also features this structure and tone: it focuses on characters who occupy the lowest positions in society and shows that these people are deprived of any opportunities for social mobility. For example, none of Ignatius's political endeavours are successful, and even when the characters win small victories, their lives do not change: they are still penniless, and are still unable to break free of the class system that is trampling them underfoot.

In other words, the novel seamlessly blends comedy and tragedy. While the characters themselves are amusing, and their bodily functions are used as the punchline for many of the novel's jokes, their overall stories end tragically. In pure comedy, which is a genre that dates back to antiquity, the main character traditionally gets a happy ending. However, this is not necessarily the case in picaresque fiction, which usually comes full circle and ends with the characters still trapped in their miserable lives.

A multi-layered narrative

The general structure of *A Confederacy of Dunces* is fairly similar to *The Consolation of Philosophy*. Both books contain chapters which are divided into sub-chapters, and follow a number of different plotlines which eventually converge to create an ending which keeps the reader on the edge of their seat. For example, certain chapters focus exclusively on Jones and his unfair working conditions, while others focus on Darlene and her dreams. This shapes the world the characters live in by providing a number of complementary perspectives on it.

However, our understanding of the novel's characters and their actions is also shaped by the other texts scattered throughout it. The story is not just told through the detached voice of the narrator, but also through the letters exchanged by Ignatius and Myrna, which provide the reader with additional insight into their relationship and their individual beliefs, as well as allowing us to learn more about Myrna's political activities and the kinds of conversations the couple used to have.

A Confederacy of Dunces also includes snippets of the novel Ignatius is writing, which is titled *The Journal of a Working Boy* and mostly consists of incendiary remarks about the society he lives in. It is both a humorous book which describes the absurdities of the world of work and a reflection of the way Ignatius's mind works, and it allows the reader to explore his worldview. This *mise en abyme* (a story which is told in the context of a wider narrative and reflects elements of its plot) could therefore be described as the nerve centre of the novel.

Furthermore, passages from *The Consolation of Philosophy* and other classic books are also included in the novel, which gives us some insight into Ignatius's literary tastes. Ignatius also discusses (and often ridicules) a number of films and TV shows which were popular at the time, which is another structural technique which allows the reader to understand his ethical, medieval inner world. This novel goes beyond a simple description of the character's actions and allows the reader to immerse themselves in his ideology and way of thinking.

THEMES

Alienation and poverty

The settings in *A Confederacy of Dunces* tend to be claustrophobic and cluttered with junk, which is usually waste from a different world that the characters never set foot in:

> "Miss Trixie's apartment was decorated with scraps, with junk, with bits of metal, with cardboard boxes. Somewhere beneath it all there was furniture. The surface, however, the visible terrain, was a landscape of old clothes and crates and newspapers. There was a pass through the center of the mountain, a clearing among the litter, a narrow aisle of clear floor [...]" (p. 371)

The characters in this novel do not just live in poverty: they accumulate it. Their possessions are worthless, and could not be exchanged for anything better. No matter what these characters do, they are defeated: most of them are unemployed, and the ones who do have jobs work in appalling conditions for meagre salaries. The city seems to be infested with misery, and no one can escape the inexorable onset of decay.

The poverty the characters live in is coupled with alienation. Most of the characters have fallen into the clutches of alcohol, television, films or underpaid jobs, and lead solitary lives in their squalid rooms or apartments with hardly anyone to talk to – and the few conversations they do have quickly devolve into squabbles. In fact, their only real communication with others is by means of technology like telephones, televisions and cinema screens.

Work

Ignatius refuses to work until his mother forces him to do so, and even then he wonders why he cannot simply sit down and write for hours on end. The only jobs he can find have meagre salaries and the work is mind-numbingly repetitive. In fact, the novel rejects the idea that work can ever be clean, fair or mentally stimulating; on the contrary, work is presented as nothing more than a trap that we are forced into by our parents, our bosses and the law.

Furthermore, none of the characters are able to use work as a means of escape or as a way of manoeuvring into a more privileged position: the only thing their jobs offer them is a means of survival. Ignatius only earns a few dollars per day, and Jones has to settle for a job as a cleaner in his own neighbourhood, as he is unable to escape the confines of the city.

There is also no escape to be found through protests or joining political parties. When Ignatius tries to organise a strike for the factory workers, he achieves nothing except his own dismissal and ridicule. He realises that organising misery leads to nothing, as there is nothing more that can be done after all the employees have already been fired.

The novel also depicts the difficulties of trying to embark on a literary career, as Ignatius never makes any money from his intelligent manuscripts. Similarly, Darlene never makes any money as a stripper, showing that neither intelligence nor physical prowess is rewarded in the dark streets of New Orleans.

Politics

The most idiosyncratic aspect of Ignatius's mindset is his political outlook. Like his religious views – he is a devout Catholic who hates the Pope – his political opinions are a jumble of contradictory positions. He frequently remarks that his preferred system of government is monarchy, but on other occasions he seems to be staunchly left-wing, and instead of longing for a return to the feudalism that is usually associated with monarchy, he supports the trade union movements organised by New Orleans's black population. Likewise, instead of closely following the strict doctrine of the Catholic Church, he tries to set up a political party for gays and lesbians.

Ignatius goes out of his way to be provocative – he even aligns himself with Myrna, who is extremely liberal, so that he can spread his reactionary ideas more easily. Above all, his political beliefs are anti-establishment: he wants to destroy the injustice, corruption and idiocy that modern society is founded on. Most of his ideology is based on the idea that society has become a den of consumerism, and that people have stopped bothering to cultivate wit and intelligence as a result.

FURTHER REFLECTION

SOME QUESTIONS TO THINK ABOUT...

- What is the significance of costumes in *A Confederacy of Dunces*?
- Write a summary of *The Journal of a Working Boy*.
- If you had to interview Ignatius, what questions would you ask him?
- Given that comparisons have often been drawn between Ignatius and Don Quixote, which character in *A Confederacy of Dunces* could be compared to Sancho Panza?
- Given that Ignatius is so critical of modernity, why do you think he watches so much television?

We want to hear from you!
Leave a comment on your online library
and share your favourite books on social media!

FURTHER READING

REFERENCE EDITION

- Kennedy Toole, J. (1987) *A Confederacy of Dunces*. New York: Grove Weidenfeld.

REFERENCE STUDIES

- Echavarría, M. F. (2009) Las enfermedades mentales según Tomás de Aquino. Sobre las enfermedades (mentales) en sentido estricto. *Abat Oliba CEU University*. [Online]. [Accessed 15 March 2018]. Available from: <http://bdigital.uncu.edu.ar/objetos_digitales/3793/03-echavarria-scripta-v3-n1.pdf>

- García, A. (2015) Las incógnitas de 'La conjura de los necios', desveladas. *El País*. [Online]. [Accessed 15 March 2018]. Available from: <http://elpais.com/elpais/2015/07/13/tentaciones/1436779957_391981.html>

- Marx, K. (2007) *Economic and Philosophic Manuscripts of 1844*. Trans. Milligan, M. New York: Dover.

RECOMMENDED READING

- Boethius, A. (2003) *The Consolation of Philosophy.* Trans. Watts, V. London: Penguin.

www.brightsummaries.com

Ebook EAN: 9782808002004

Paperback EAN: 9782808002011

Legal Deposit: D/2017/12603/621

Cover: © Primento

Digital conception by Primento, the digital partner of publishers.

15813427R00032

Printed in Great Brit
by Amazon